# USS NEW JERSEY

## WORLD WAR II
## TO THE
## PERSIAN GULF

PHOTOGRAPHY BY NEIL LEIFER          TEXT BY ROBERT F. DORR

MBI Publishing Company

This edition published in 2002 by MBI Publishing Company, Galtier Plaza, Suite 200, 380 Jackson Street, St. Paul, MN 55101-3885 USA

MBI Publishing Company books are also available at discounts in bulk quantity for industrial or sales-promotional use. For details write to Special Sales Manager at Motorbooks International Wholesalers & Distributors, Galtier Plaza, Suite 200, 380 Jackson Street, St. Paul, MN 55101-3885 USA.

Library of Congress Cataloging-in-Publication Data Available

ISBN 0-7603-1207-9

**On the front cover:** Fire One! The big guns launched 16-inch shells that weighed 2,700 pounds each and had a range of over 18 miles. *Neil Leifer*

**On the frontispiece:** A dramatic head-on view of the massive ship as it heads across the Pacific bound for Southeast Asia. The powerful, 887.6-foot-long battleship was capable of top speeds of 34 knots. *Neil Leifer*

**On the title page:** The *USS New Jersey* passes through the Panama Canal with its crew "manning the rail" in their dress whites for the special occasion. *Neil Leifer*

**On the contents page:** As the *USS New Jersey* was removed from mothballs, one of its two 17-foot, 5-bladed inboard propellers was moved by a work crew in 1967. The ship also had two 18.25-foot, 4-bladed outboard propellers. *Neil Leifer*

**On the back cover,** *top*: Using a combination of elbow grease and "spit and polish," the crew keeps the *New Jersey*—including its impressive wooden deck—in immaculate condition. *Neil Leifer*
*bottom*: Fireboats spray their salute as the reborn battleship leaves Philadelphia in April 1968. *Neil Leifer*

Printed in China

# Contents

# Battlewagon

The battleship evokes a special awe. At once graceful and powerful, the mighty dreadnought has no peer for her impressive size, her withering firepower, and the richness of color and fury when her guns let loose.

When the United States Navy decided to bring one of these majestic vessels back into service as a seaborne artillery platform for the Vietnam War, the Fleet acquired a most impressive warship. USS *New Jersey* (BB-62) was the second of six ships planned in the *Iowa* class, of which four were actually completed. Displacing 45,000 tons at rest and 58,000 under way with a full load, these were the largest battleships ever to sail on the world's oceans, with the exception of two unsuccessful Japanese dreadnoughts.

Construction of the first two in the series had been authorized on May 17, 1938, and *Iowa* (BB-61), *New Jersey*, *Missouri* (BB-63) and *Wisconsin* (BB-64) all established excellent combat records in the maritime struggle against Japan, although two further battlewagons in the class, *Kentucky* and *Illinois*, were still being built on VJ Day.

While *Missouri* was backed in Congress by a then-little-known senator named Harry S. Truman, and ultimately became host to the Japanese surrender in Tokyo Bay in 1945, over a longer span of years *New Jersey* saw the most service of any ship in her class and, more importantly, became the world's most famous battleship.

"This ship has a mystique," noted Captain J. Edward Snyder, Jr., who drew the envied task of commanding the vessel on its return not merely to life but to war. (The job was so coveted that in an earlier era a rear admiral happily gave up his stars in order to become skipper of the battleship.)

*New Jersey* was, in fact, the second capital ship to bear the name. Snyder's simple evocation of the ship's mystique, the yearning of the seagoing man for a more romantic past, traces back to a proud December morning in 1907 when Teddy Roosevelt saluted the sixteen battleships of his Great White Fleet, the original *New Jersey* among them, as they stood out from Hampton Roads at the start of a triumphant world tour. That first warship bearing the name of the Garden State was sunk in 1922 as target practice for Billy Mitchell's experimental bombers, the very act of

*continued on page 8*

"Enthusiasm" is the word for spirits on board a battleship, including those of a sailor communicating with a replenishment ship via a method invented before radio and radar. Battle stars from numerous Pacific campaigns appear behind this signalman, as well as the Republic of Korea *taeguki* (national flag) from more recent campaigns.

*continued from page 6*
which convinced many that the era of the battleship was history.

Laid down on September 16, 1940, and launched on August 27, 1942, under the sponsorship of Carolyn Edison, wife of New Jersey's governor (and using twenty-six tons of grease to slide down the ways at Philadelphia Navy Yard), BB-62 seemed to signal that even if battlewagons were no longer the capital ships of any navy—no one could deny the ascendancy of the aircraft carrier—they nonetheless possessed an enormity and force all their own. Commissioned on May 23, 1943, *New Jersey* took those sixteen-inch guns to war, continuing both the mystique and the legacy. Flying the flags of naval task force Commanders Spruance and Halsey, she carried the battle to Kwajelein, Eniwetok, the Carolinas, Saipan, Luzon, Iwo Jima, Okinawa, Truk and, finally, to Tokyo harbor.

Mothballed on June 30, 1948, *New Jersey* was brought forth once more for conflict in Korea. Commissioned for the second time on November 21, 1950, she fought valiantly until, once again, she was deemed excess to the Navy's needs. On August 21, 1957,

*continued on page 12*

"Manning the rail" brings the crew out in dress whites. It's a formal event, and it's appropriate for passing through the Panama Canal. When the original specifications for the *Iowa*-class battleships were set forth on June 9, 1938, one provision was that the vessel had to fit through the canal.

Photographer Neil Leifer gets comfortable on *New Jersey*'s bow. Neil was twenty-six when *New Jersey* was recommissioned for Vietnam, and had already been taking pictures and building ship models for many years.

*Next page*
Men file aboard *New Jersey* on March 19, 1968, for her Southeast Asia cruise. The battlewagon was no Hilton hotel, and seamen had to make do with the contents of a duffle bag, a narrow bunk and a small personal locker. The relatively small size of the crew during this period allowed for considerable space within the vessel, however, and The Big J was considered not merely a prestigious ship to serve on, but a comfortable one.

*continued from page 8*

*New Jersey* was put to sleep for the second time. Missiles, submarines and nuclear-powered warships were on the Navy's shopping list of modern technology. Battleships? Snyder had not yet had a chance to make his point, but throughout most of the 1960s, battleships were ignored. Still, the dreadnought's mystique survived.

The 1967-68 resurrection of *New Jersey* for the Vietnam War is the subject of the photo essay which follows, taking the mighty battleship from mothballs in Philadelphia to combat in the South China Sea. It was a time of promise and hope, and few could have believed that this great gray lady would appear only briefly in the combat zone. *New Jersey* performed with success and valor, and her guns brought incomparable devastation down on the heads of the Viet Cong and North Vietnamese. It remains a puzzle why she was not kept on duty into the heavy

*continued on page 16*

On a hot day, some of the metal could be sizzling to the touch. Most of it was too thick to become very hot, however, the ship having been designed with armor in an era when men expected that battlewagons would trade gunfire with each other. Though she slept for a long time, much as this sailor dozes aft of the gun turrets, *New Jersey* had a reputation as a happy ship when she was resurrected for Vietnam. For the Southeast Asia cruise, ship's crew was seventy officers and 1,556 men, roughly half the number who crewed her in World War II.

Among the first things to be refurbished when the battleship comes out of mothballs: the plaque honoring the early history of *New Jersey* and the predecessor ship of the same name.

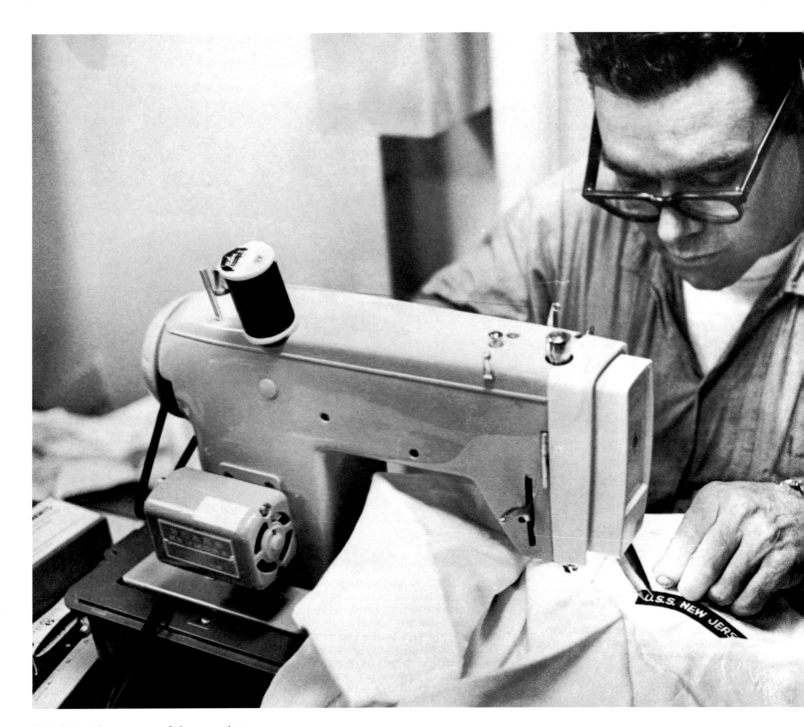

Stitching the name of the newly recommissioned ship on Class B whites makes it official. Bringing *New Jersey* out of mothballs is only half the job; a crew must be made ready as well. Although the Navy claimed that every man aboard The Big J was a volunteer, in fact only about ten percent truly were. Still, morale was high and the sailors believed that once they arrived in the combat zone their devastating firepower would make a difference.

"Ready down below?" With sea trials about to begin, some of the equipment aboard *New Jersey*, including the intercom used by this petty officer, is little-changed from two wars ago.

15

*continued from page 12*

fighting of 1972 when she could have made an even greater contribution.

Though her Vietnam era ended—prematurely, most believed—with decommissioning on December 17, 1969, in a very real sense, *New Jersey*'s story is as poignant and graphic as today's headlines.

A strong proponent of battleships for today's world, defense consultant Charles E. Myers, Jr., published an article in November 1979 calling for re-activation of the *Iowa*-class warships yet another time. Vietnam lay behind, but the seizure of hostages at the US Embassy in Tehran that month symbolized America's difficulty in projecting power. The Carter Administration was lukewarm toward Myers' idea but in January 1981 the newly elected Ronald Reagan and Navy Secretary John Lehman took notice. Myers convinced both men that in the 1980s battleships could employ their unique firepower effectively and wield a newer generation of weapons, such as the *Tomahawk* cruise missile.

And so, *New Jersey* experienced yet another rebirth. Her modern period began with the ship's fourth commissioning ceremony on December 28, 1982. United

These two views of The Big J from straight ahead, taken during sea trials near Philadelphia as the ship awaited commissioning on April 6, 1968, illustrate how unwise it would be to have the battleship coming on from dead-ahead. More than once, Soviet trawlers and spy ships tried to cut abruptly across *New Jersey*'s bow, only to narrowly escape harm. Displacing 58,000 tons with a full load, the battlewagon simply pushed aside anything in front of it.

States policy had become, in effect, to regard the battleship as a capital warship in exactly the same way the aircraft carrier was regarded. Critics argued that the ship could not be fully manned with the number of sailors available to the all-volunteer force of the eighties; they cited the age of the ship and the high cost of recommissioning.

Bent on achieving a 600-ship navy with fifteen carrier battle groups—several of these headed up by a battleship rather than a carrier—the Reagan Administration ignored the critics and forged ahead. The 1980s have seen *New Jersey* lobbing shells into Beirut and, more recently, guarding US interests in the Persian Gulf.

In a world of "low intensity conflict," the Pentagon's new jargon for limited war, government policy on big battleships has changed. In contrast with the Vietnam era when the word "austere" was used repeatedly to describe the program for resurrecting the *New Jersey,* big has become the byword, and the capacity of a battlewagon for decisive action in a limited conflict is recognized. In the Reagan era, instead of the austere Vietnam period, a major investment was made in new weapons, new electronics and new systems. Sister ship *Iowa* joined the Fleet, too, although she was absent from the Vietnam War. *Missouri* and *Wisconsin* remain in mothballs, but attention has been given to their condition in recent years in recognition of possibly bringing them to life yet again. In the 1980s, *Iowa* and *New Jersey* are likely to remain in service.

The mighty guns were the trademark of this massive, colorful ship but her finely constructed wooden deck also required considerable care and attention. A proud crew using a fair amount of spit and polish managed to keep both guns and deck spotless, causing one admiral to remark that the dreadnought was the best-maintained vessel in the fleet.

*Next page*
The gray ship often found itself moving through a sea so blue the depth of color provoked the brain. The sixteen-inch guns were billed as "Firepower for Freedom," but it was always men, like this helmeted sailor peering into binoculars, who made the difference.

The battle insignia E for efficiency was not easily earned. Though there were differences of opinion over her role in the Vietnam War, there was never any doubt that *New Jersey* was a taut, battle-ready ship. Those who gave the award agreed.

*Previous page*
It took hard heads and hardhats to bring *New Jersey* out of dormancy at Philadelphia and restore her as a fighting vessel.

# Out of mothballs

The Vietnam War was tailor-made for the size and striking power of the battleship. Most of North Vietnam's infiltration of the south was taking place along coastal routes easily within range of naval artillery. Some targets in Ho Chi Minh's homeland seemed to have been designed with *New Jersey* in mind: The Thanh Hoa bridge (also known as the Dragon's Jaw), crossing the Song Ma River south of Hanoi, stubbornly refused to bend or break after repeated air strikes over a period of more than three years. Captain Snyder quickly pointed out to his superiors that a barrage from The Big J's guns would crumple the bridge in minutes. As he prepared to go to war in early 1968, however, Snyder did not know that *New Jersey* would arrive in the battle zone just as Lyndon Johnson declared a halt to striking targets north of the 19th Parallel.

There were still plenty of targets in the south, however. Nothing, not even a B-52 strike, compared with the noise, the ferocity and the devastation

*continued on next page*

*New Jersey* in dry dock in Philadelphia, December 7, 1967.

25

*continued from page 25*

wreaked by those sixteen-inchers. *New Jersey* would be able to use its firepower very effectively.

The Navy had originally wanted to bring all four *Iowa*-class battleships out of mothballs. Opposition was strong among the top brass, particularly in the naval aviation community. When only one battleship could be brought back to service, *New Jersey* was the obvious choice. She had been re-gunned prior to leaving service in 1957. She was in relatively good condition under her cocoon of protective coating at the Philadelphia Navy Yard. An official estimate held that recommissioning work could be carried out at Philadelphia's Dry Dock Number 3 in a nine-month period for $24 million, a modest sum under the circumstances.

A slumbering giant, *New Jersey* awaited the jackhammers, welder's torches and rivet guns that would bring her back to life. The decision had been made to employ the battleship solely for shore bombardment, so her new configuration was to be an austere one. In fact, the word austere got so much

*continued on page 29*

Gray ship, gray day. Scaffolding has been partially erected as work proceeds at the Philadelphia Navy Yard. Fully one-half of the dreadnought's hull lies beneath the surface when she sails with a full load, so in dry dock the ship appears larger than ever. In fact, elaborate safety precautions were made to prevent workers from falling.

continued from page 26
attention among men tasked to restore the ship cheaply that the captain's mess on this non-alcoholic American vessel soon boasted a simple drink made from apples called "austerity punch."

The sixteen-inch and secondary five-inch guns were revitalized for the new mission. But the Vietnam-era configuration did not include an elaborate electronics refit, vertical takeoff aircraft or missiles.

With no small amount of effort, *New Jersey* was eased into Philadelphia's Dry Dock Number 3 on September 20, 1967, to begin the arduous refitting process. A major problem with an outboard deck lug for the Number 1 sixteen-inch gun turret was resolved with some fancy dog-robbing which included acquiring the needed item from the Army's Aberdeen Proving Ground.

As hundreds of yard workers embarked on the restoration effort they were encouraged to find that the battlewagon was well-preserved. Her boilers required little work, the quality of her finely burnished teak wood decks had not changed with age, and a surprising

continued on page 34

The "mothballs" were in fact a protective material which was easily removed, but the full job of bringing the ship out of mothballs was to involve thousands of hours of effort by hundreds of yard workers. Work on the spinners for the ship's giant propellers proved to be a real challenge.

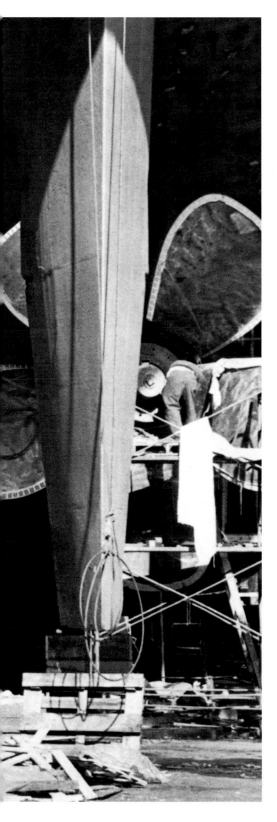

BB-62's four giant propellers, in pairs of slightly different sizes, required a major refurbishing effort. So, too, did work on the stern of the giant dreadnought as she lay in dry dock.

*Next page*
On November 27, 1967, early work is under way on *New Jersey's* main battery turrets, while workers prepare to remove the 40-mm gun tub located atop turret Number 2.

*continued from page 29*
number of spare parts was still readily available in Navy inventory.

During refitting work in Philadelphia, *New Jersey*'s skipper-designate was asked to give up his coveted slot. Captain Richard G. Alexander had become involved in a media issue, the Arnheiter affair, speaking publicly in defense of Commander Marcus Aurelius Arnheiter who'd been relieved of command for eccentric behavior while skipper of a destroyer-escort, USS *Vance* (DER-387). Because of his outspoken defense of a former shipmate, Captain Alexander ended up turning The Big J over to Captain Snyder, a classmate at the Naval Academy, Annapolis, in 1945, and a fellow advocate of the battleship.

Bringing the big gray ship out of mothballs was a massive undertaking which required the skills of workers from an engine room expert to a painter. *New Jersey* was a most imposing sight in dry dock, and the ship stood so high that many working on

*continued on page 38*

*Following pages*
Engines, boilers and bulkheads were in remarkably good shape after years in mothballs. Though a clerical force of sixteen people was occupied tracking down more than 160,000 spare parts for *New Jersey*, ranging from valves to rangefinders, the workforce found it reasonable to cope with the ship's piping, decking and, above all, the mighty sixteen-inch Mark Two naval guns which had been newly installed just before the vessel's 1957 retirement.

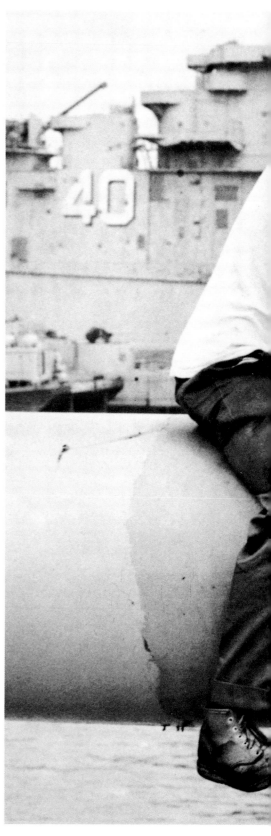

*continued from page 34*
her, whether above or below, experienced vertigo.

The first priority was to ensure that BB-62 would have a smoothly functioning main battery. The sixteen-inchers were cleaned and reworked. The huge projectiles fired by these guns were carefully inspected and updated. Two Mark 48 fire-control computers were among new items installed, despite the emphasis on austerity. Provisions were made for fork lifts aboard the ship to handle the 2,700-pound shells fired by the guns.

Removing an unwanted item, the crane hoists away one of the six cupola-style covers which protected the battleship while she was in retirement.

Waiting to be brought to life, *New Jersey* is still in mothballs in this early view which accents her enormous firepower.

Did fate pick an ironic date—January 23, 1968—for the application of *New Jersey*'s hull number? This also happened to be the day the US intelligence ship *Pueblo* was seized by North Korea, an event which probably could not have occurred had a battleship been anywhere within a few hundred nautical miles. Acrylic, salt-resistant paint was used to complete the eight-foot 62 on the bow of BB-62. The painter was dwarfed by the imposing size of the ship and its main anchor.

## Following pages

Her *raison d'etre* was to employ guns at long range and with great force against an enemy, and every feature of the battleship's design was intended toward this purpose. But *New Jersey* was something else, too—one of the marvels of man's industrial age. Though she may appear dated to today's post-industrial eyes, the mighty dreadnought was an extraordinary assemblage of heavy iron at a time when making big, heavy and complex machines was seen as the pinnacle of human endeavor. It is very likely that no future warship will ever be as massive as *New Jersey,* for she came into being at a time when size itself was a measure of achievement.

The months of labor and love that brought the dreadnought out from the mothballs came to a culmination with formal commissioning of *New Jersey* at the Philadelphia piers on a sun-splashed Saturday, April 6, 1968. A group of anti-war demonstrators hovered at the fringe of the event, which culminated with Captain Snyder turning away from the crew on board to address their families on the pier. The final work on the ship had been a stem-to-stern cleaning for the occasion which left *New Jersey* in pristine condition. The raising of the flag—the first time *New Jersey* had borne the colors of all fifty states—reflected the feelings of all who had brought the ship to Fleet status and would take it to war. These were feelings of pride and purpose, and above all the sense of belonging to a special vessel, the world's only active battleship at the time.

# Men, ship, sea

On March 26, 1968, *New Jersey* slid out from her Philadelphia berthing and steamed down the Delaware River for engineering trials. Captain Snyder puffed on his ubiquitous pipe while directing events from the bridge and circulating throughout the vessel to observe how his confined community hummed and purred, coping with any unexpected snags. A sea shakedown of the battleship's engines was carried out successfully. *New Jersey* was ticking like a Swiss watch; from the luxury guest billet known as the Halsey Suite to the depths of the engine room, everything was running perfectly. Throughout the ship, checklists were "signed off" and when completed the battleship returned to her berth with a broom run up a signal halyard—the time-honored symbol that muster had been passed and a "clean sweep" achieved.

On April 6, 1968, battleship BB-62 was re-commissioned with many guests in attendance and much festive pomp. The Road Runner caricature was painted on a fairing in the engine room while an ordnanceman had scribbled "No joy for Hanoi" on the shell feeder yoke of one of the sixteen-inch guns.

The colorful and happy occasion was marred by two events earlier that week. The first was President Lyndon Johnson's surprise April 1 announcement that he would place all but the southern panhandle of North Vietnam off limits for bombing and shelling in the hope of furthering peace negotiations. And the second was the assassination of Martin Luther King on April 4.

The latter event sparked racial disturbances in Philadelphia, and the commissioning was also attended by a small but vocal cadre of anti-war protestors. Still, Captain Snyder and his crew felt that this formal rebirth of the *New Jersey* was a poignant and special event, and the men hoped and believed that they would make a contribution to the war effort.

*continued on page 54*

Ready for seas, although not yet fully loaded with sixteen-inch projectiles for her nine main battery guns, *New Jersey* is seen off by families of the crew. The ship's five-inch guns, making up her secondary battery, are raised to maximum angle.

*Next page*
Farewell to Philadelphia. Two of the four tugs needed to steer the mighty battleship from pierside to center channel in the Delaware River are retiring from the scene as fireboats send up cascades to mark BB-62's departure. Two sister *Iowa*-class battleships, still in mothballs, remain while The Big J's crew mans the rails and the ship heads out.

*continued from page 51*

Manning the rails in dress whites, the crew said goodbye to Philadelphia. *New Jersey* put to sea and sailed for Norfolk, Virginia, to take on ammunition, winching aboard dozens of the huge sixteen-inch shells. Her passage through the Panama Canal followed—a tight fit, indeed—and after a visit to Long Beach, California, on June 11, 1968, a six-week period of workups and gunnery practice followed off the California coast. On August 2, 1968, The Big J was back in port at Long Beach for final yard work before embarking. September 5, 1968, saw a poignant farewell to the west coast as the crew went aboard *New Jersey,* said more goodbyes, and set sail for the real thing—the war zone.

The metal-gray interiors and work areas of the ship became as familiar to each man as the back of his hand. Each had a place to belong inside the great iron canyon of the ship, whether in the plotting rooms with the subdued red light and annotated maps, or in a powder magazine with the enclosed constraints and

*continued on page 57*

*New Jersey*'s executive officer, or XO, keeps a critical watch on events while the ship plows through the sea. While the captain's leadership is the final test of a good ship, the XO probably has the most difficult job on board, overseeing the heads of divisions throughout the vessel. A helmet is part of combat gear normally donned only during General Quarters.

*Previous page*
Riding high in a calm sea, *New Jersey* precedes the sun. Just below the surface and not seen in this view is the forefoot, the bulbous fairing where the stern meets the keel at the bottom of the bow.

Re-arming at sea. Powder bags were every bit as important as the bullets and, while not as heavy, were often more difficult to handle. A canister of powder used to fire the ship's gun projectiles is wheeled with care across the largest wooden deck in the Navy.

*continued from page 54*

peculiar acrid smell, or in the long third-deck passageway which passed beneath the bridge between turrets 2 and 3, and was called Broadway because of the heavy foot-traffic it handled. The warrant officers had the misfortune of being billeted just aft of turret 2, so that gunnery practice made sleep impossible for those off duty. "Officer country" provided the most commodious living space but was also the scene of the most flurry and movement. *New Jersey* had a closed-circuit television system, the biggest laundry room of any vessel afloat, a major medical facility and dozens of other workplaces to support her real purpose—firing the guns.

Manning the mighty ship while under way at sea was a challenge to all hands, and the crew responded with zest and vigor. The skipper set the tone, and on this ship there was a happy approach to hard work. The captain was the example with long hours of grueling "hands on" effort broken by

*continued on page 60*

*Left & following pages*

Piloting *New Jersey* through the Panama Canal was no easy feat. Officially, a vessel with a beam of 108 feet was passing through locks 110-feet wide, but sailors divined that these numbers were deceptive. It was, in fact, such a close shave that six-inch drain nozzles protruding from the side of the vessel were flattened or temporarily removed to make *New Jersey* thin enough. At some points along the canal the squeeze was so tight that lookouts posted along the hull could scarcely see where the ship ended and the canal began.

*continued from page 57*

lighter moments when he shared ice cream with the lower ratings and circulated among the crew, sharing conversation and camaraderie. The Old Man deigned to exact stern discipline when needed, showed compassion when appropriate. The exec bore the task of whipping departments into shape with a similar mixture of firmness and humor. As the mighty vessel plowed westward, all hands were aware that they would soon be on the gunline facing Vietnam.

An enlisted seaman faced all the rigors of the sea that have challenged navymen from time immemorial. A work shift might begin at dusk or dawn, the ship a twenty-four-hour concern, the duties of the men as varied as the work of hundreds of people in a small city. Instruments had to be calibrated, guns cleaned and inspected, the radar watch maintained, the boilers tended, bread baked for around-the-clock meal servings. Ammunition handlers worked at accelerating the speed at which they could load a sixteen-inch gun—safely—until it took less than a minute to load a projectile and powder bag.

*New Jersey* was fortunate in having a respected cadre of old-salt chief petty officers who spoke the language of men and machines, and who exerted real leadership. Periods of frenetic activity were interrupted by an occasional respite. The traditional and rather prankish shellback party was an event which bolstered spirts at the crossing of the equator.

A port call at Subic Bay, the mighty bastion in the Philippines, gave the men their last visit ashore before swinging into action.

On the morning of September 30, 1968, *New Jersey* hove-to fourteen miles off the Chu Lai peninsula and was called to General Quarters. Her first target was an enemy supply dump just north of the Ben Hai River which bisected the grossly misnamed Demilitarized Zone (DMZ) between North and South Vietnam. The guns were elevated, the alarm klaxon was sounded, and *New Jersey*'s turret 2 fired its first shot in anger. The pilot of the Marine TA-4F Skyhawk "calling" the target quickly radioed adjustments, and a brief bombardment wiped out every last vestige of the enemy dump. *New Jersey* and her men had reached the gunline.

*Next page*
Whether it was a successful canal passage or a port call, spirits were always high aboard *New Jersey*. Navy men always felt a special attachment to this ship. Some, who served on a number of vessels in their careers, always insisted that their tour aboard BB-62 was the standard by which all other naval experiences were measured.

Wooden decks, big guns and dedicated sailors: These were the ingredients which made *New Jersey* such an inspiring sight wherever she went. When under way on sea maneuvers, the crew rarely assembled topside, but when transiting friendly waters it was customary to man the rails, even if informally.

In "Command," the ship's command control center, or Triple-C, men use radar and electronic data to maintain close watch on the tactical situation. Plotting of other vessels, aircraft and shore activity is crucial to readiness for battle. Communication between the bridge, the separate combat information center ("Combat") and the ship's gun positions is a continuing process.

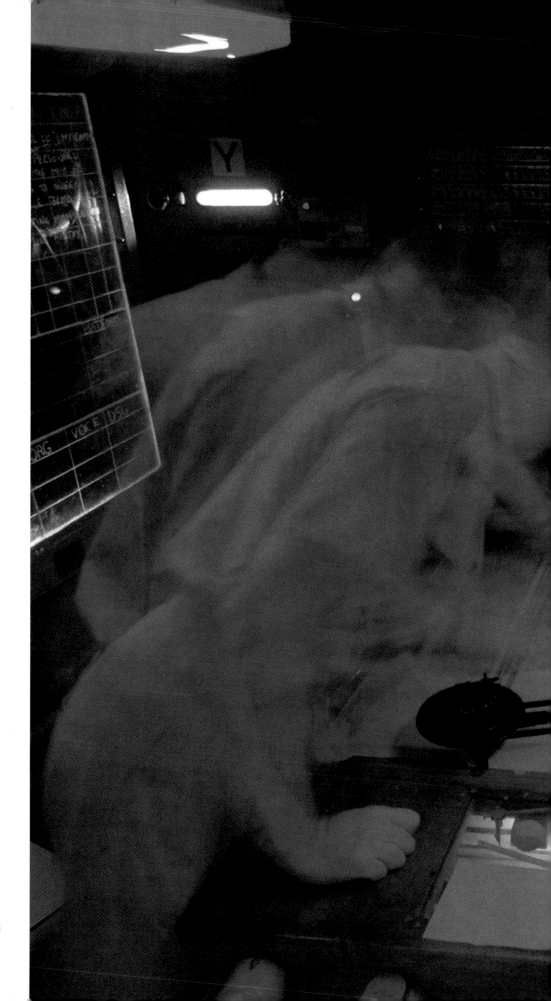

The pace of activity in Triple-C is stepped up when the ship is "on the line" sailing off a hostile coast and likely to be called upon to use her guns.

*Previous page*
On the gunline, *New Jersey* rarely
traveled alone. Cruisers, frigates
and destroyers were usually on
duty to help with naval gunfire
missions against coastal targets.
Here, a transfer of supplies from
the smaller vessel is about to take
place. Despite the heavy seas,
BB-62 will fire a line across to the
escorting destroyer USS *Towers*
(DDG-9).

The smaller vessel is the recipient
of the highline which will carry
mail, food or supplies across open
water to *New Jersey*. In choppy
seas, sailors had an unusually
difficult time making the transfer
work.

Even the mightiest of machines must rely, in order to function, on the muscles of men. The dreadnought's sailors tug hard to bring the highline into place for a ship-to-ship transfer which can take place while at full steam.

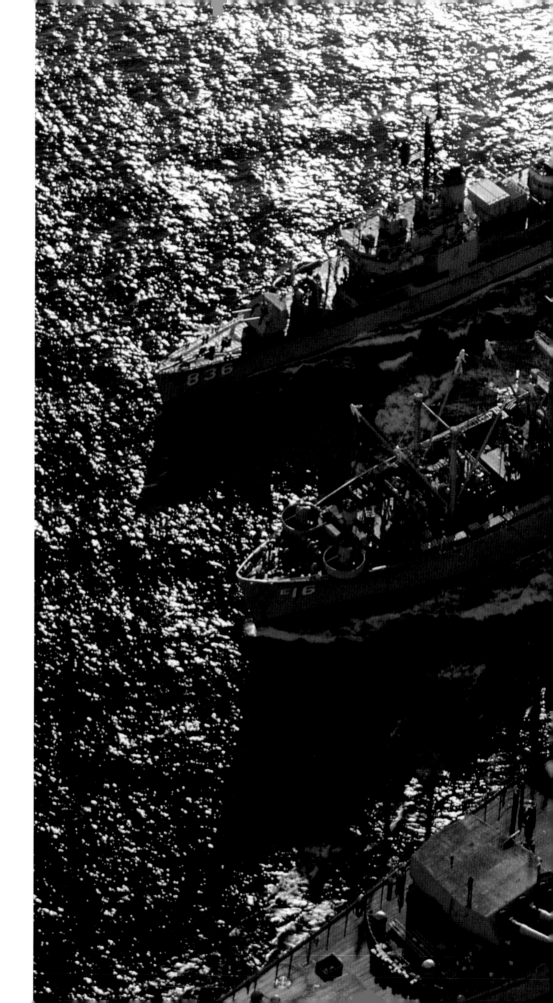

Transfer more often involves a
tender or supply vessel and can
include three or more ships at
once.

*Previous page*
Once the job is done, there may be
time for a brief rest—here, in a sea
of hardhats—but not for long.

There is never a time not to be
vigilant.

# Big guns

"**W**elcome to the war," was the message radioed by the pilot of that first Skyhawk to act as a spotter plane for *New Jersey*.

Wielding her big guns against North Vietnamese concentrations eleven miles north of the DMZ on October 1, 1968, the battleship returned the welcome when another Skyhawk was hit by ground fire while acting as the ship's eyes. Alert sailors in *New Jersey*'s combat information center (CIC) kept tabs on the two-man crew and guided the plane out from the coast until both men ejected almost directly overhead and were handily rescued by the escorting destroyer USS *Towers*.

While skipper and crew dealt decisively with this event and with the other chores of war—the men were ever-alert

*continued on next page*

Although no warship in the fleet had used them for more than a decade, a sufficient number of sixteen-inch projectiles remained in stock to keep *New Jersey* adequately supplied. Handling the mighty bullets was another proposition. The men needed carts, capstans, hoists and a significant amount of Mark One Arm Muscle.

for North Vietnamese P-4 patrol boats or *Osa*-class fast attack vessels although Ho Chi Minh's sailors never rose to the challenge—*New Jersey* directed further day and night gunfire north of the DMZ.

Near dusk on October 7, 1968, shallow-bottom enemy vessels were spotted paralleling the North Vietnamese coast near the Song Giang River. *New Jersey* and *Towers* engaged with five-inch naval guns and destroyed eleven. But it was always the larger sixteen-inch naval guns which captured the imagination of everyone associated with the great battlewagon. From the bridge to CIC, from Command to the plotting boards, from Broadway to turret 1, every man on the vessel felt that his sweat, his toil and his determination were personified in those mighty sixteen-inch projectiles. *New Jersey* was many things to many people, but above all she was big guns.

The journey traveled by those sixteen-inch projectiles, from reaching the battleship until reaching an enemy target, was a full-fledged

*continued on page 83*

An overhead look at the gun deck shows the trail the projectiles follow as they are moved from a neat row via handcart to the hoist located atop turret 1, which lowers them onto the projectile platform below decks at the turret barbette. While on the gunline, the skipper authorized T-shirts in place of denim jackets to emphasize *New Jersey*'s role not as a floating showpiece but as a working battleship.

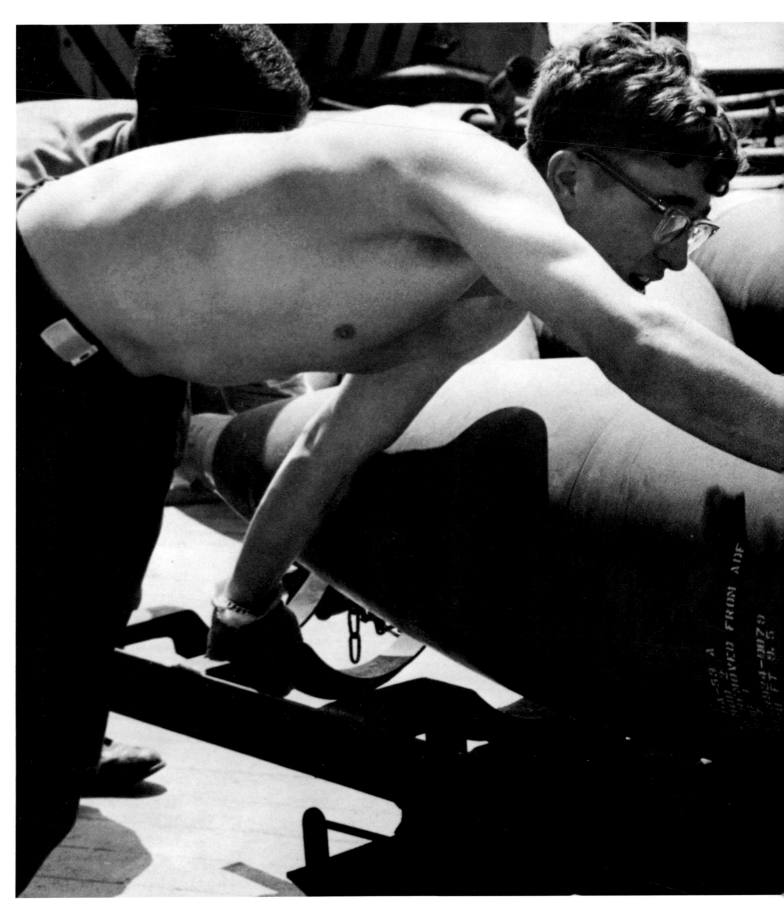

*continued from page 81*
challenge to the battleship's
two best assets, muscles and
machines. Both were needed
to handle the shells' enormous
weight.

The huge naval artillery
projectile, or bullet as
crewmen sometimes called it,
reached the battlewagon at
pierside where shells from the
Naval Ammunition Depot
were taken on—or while
under way, when an
ammunition ship such as USS
*Haleakala* (AE-25) transferred
projectiles via ship-to-ship
highline. Whether from shore
or from another ship, the
arrival of the 1,900-pound shell
(2,700 pounds with associated
powder bag) required a
motivated and well-led team
of deckhands to attend to the
loading process.

Obviously, given their
great size and bulk, each shell
had to be loaded aboard
individually. Once on the
battleship's wooden deck after
arriving via highline or crane,
the shell was then hooked up
to a small integral hoist located
on the turret. Sailors laboring
on deck eased the projectile
until its pointed, bullet shape
was aimed skyward, enabling
it to be lowered into the
depths of the great battleship
through a main deck scuttle—
in essence, a round open

*continued on page 85*

Every move with the main battery
projectiles requires some kind of
assist to the bodily toil of sailors
handling the big warheads, but
considerable "body language"
must be applied nonetheless. This
shell is being moved toward the
hoist which will place it beneath
turret 1.

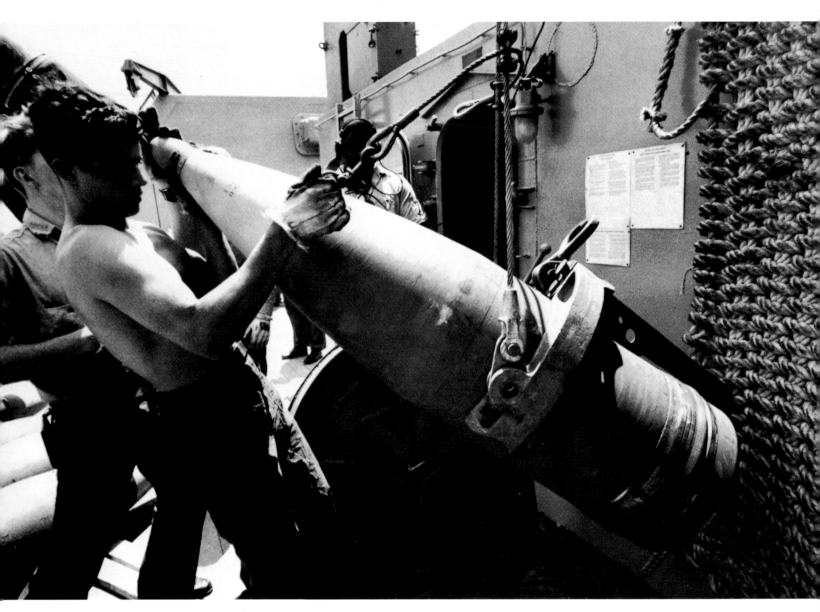

The projectile is now ready to be swung into the vertical position to be lowered through the open hatch to the projectile platform. Precautions are taken to avoid any movement with the projectile that is not intended and the men's work is carefully scrutinized by a petty officer.

*continued from page 83*
hatch of not much greater diameter than the shell itself. Next, the seamen operating the turret hoist lowered the mighty warhead into a projectile deck located beneath the turret. At every stage of movement, some form of power assist did much of the work, but the positioning of the sixteen-inch shell could not be accomplished without the strenuous labor of men.

Once inside the battleship and stowed on the projectile deck, moving one of the mighty shells even a few inches or feet was a major chore. The men kept projectile decks well-oiled to aid their manual and mechanical efforts in handling and moving each weighty bullet. Gunner's mates used a power-driven rotating capstan (in effect, a man-operated vertical winch) with a segment of line to pull, beg and cajole the projectile across the oiled metal deck in a move-by-move effort called parbuckling.

When a fire mission was called, the hard-working crews moved projectile rounds from the projectile flat in the turret barbette and raised them by elevator to the turret. The shell

*continued on next page*

Once the projectiles loaded aboard at Norfolk required replenishment, BB-62 took ammunition on board via highline transfer at sea. The shells were always defused while being handled so there was no danger of explosion. In fact, sailors considered the canisters of powder used to fire the projectiles as far more hazardous than the bullets themselves.

*continued from page 85*

was then ready to be placed into the gun breech. Behind the shell went a powder bag almost the size of the shell itself, and at its bottom a red-colored ignition pad covering the black powder into which the gun's primer was fired. By the time *New Jersey* confronted an enemy target in Vietnam, gun captains and ordnancemen reduced the difficult loading process down to the point where a new shell could be fired every forty or fifty seconds.

When a salvo of shells went into the air wrapped in a wreath of flame, it was almost certain to mean serious trouble for the North Vietnamese. Most targets were positively identified by spotter aircraft such as the ubiquitous Skyhawks and an infrequent Air Force O-2 Skymaster, but *New Jersey* also carried out H & I (harassment and interdiction) fire against targets picked in advance which could be hit at night and in bad weather.

Designed to trade crushing salvoes with enemy battleships in the midst of a raging naval battle, *New Jersey* could wield its big guns to a range and accuracy far exceeding the needs of the

*continued on page 88*

Once brought aboard, the projectiles are laid on deck awaiting the turret hoist. Planks underneath are used to facilitate movement and also protect the ship's deck. The glaring tropical sun makes the work hot and strenuous. Rolling the projectile may seem an all-too-obvious method, but it works.

continued from page 86
tactical situation in Vietnam. It almost never happened that shells from the mighty vessel missed their intended destination or went astray.

But the great accuracy of the battleship's big guns was only a part of the story. Hurled by powder blast through the rifled bore of the sixteen-inch gun and sent rushing skyward until brought down by gravity on top of its target, the projectile possessed greater penetrating power and explosive force than any other ordnance in use in Vietnam.

Many times, *New Jersey* engaged reinforced North Vietnamese bunkers which were, in effect, fortresses, and could not be touched by Marine field artillery. North Vietnam's own artillery pieces on the other side of the DMZ defied efforts by B-52s and Marine guns to put them out of business, but *New Jersey* shut them down with alacrity.

Howling down from overhead with the sound of an arriving express train, a *New Jersey* sixteen-incher could turn a heavy concrete roof into powder. It could spray blast and shrapnel for hundreds of yards; the concussion could kill a man a thousand yards away. When coupled with the

continued on next page

Once the weight of the projectile is shifted to the hoist harness, much manhandling must still be used to move the warhead to upright position. Projectiles are later stored in this position beneath the turret. Elevators will move the sixteen-inchers up to the gun breech when a firing exercise is under way.

talents of a skilled forward observer, a barrage of "incoming" from *New Jersey* had the sheer force of nothing else on earth short of an atomic explosion.

Marines cringing on the ground awaiting help from sixteen-inch "incoming" saw that *New Jersey*'s guns illuminated the sky like a false dawn. An Air Force O-2 Skymaster pilot remembers when those shells caught more than 300 North Vietnamese regular troops and plastered them against a hillside: "It was a new lesson in horror, color, carnage and lethality." The sixteen-inch shells could open up a crater fifty-five feet across, twenty feet deep.

On November 25, 1968, *New Jersey* had her biggest day of the war thus far, near Quang Nai, carrying out no fewer than eight separate fire missions with the sixteen-inch guns and destroying 117 North Vietnamese structures. The huge projectiles set off furious secondary fires. The most severe restrictions on attacking targets in North Vietnam were in effect at this time, and not a few naval officers pondered how

*continued from page 91*

Less publicized but vital to the huge ship's role as a floating gun platform are the ten five-inch batteries arrayed along the port and starboard of the vessel. Although less impressive than the dreadnought's main battery, the five-inchers by themselves provide more firepower than is found on other warships. These projectiles, at least, can be handled by a lone sailor, but not without much huffing and puffing.

continued from page 89
different things might be if the restrictions were lifted. *New Jersey* continued to wield her enormous firepower into December and—with a brief respite and a Bob Hope show on board—into the new year. Damage assessments continued to show that the ship was inflicting serious damage on the enemy, but the raising of the restrictions was not to occur for *New Jersey*.

In January 1969, *New Jersey's* main batteries provided gunfire support for Operation Bold Mariner, a partly amphibious move against major enemy forces by US Marines. Another brief respite followed, with departure from the gunline and a trip to Japan. By mid-February *New Jersey* was back, lobbing sixteen-inch shells to support Marine operations near Con Thien.

February 22, 1969, stands as perhaps the premier day of *New Jersey's* combat tour. A Marine DMZ outpost known as Oceanview and manned by only twenty Marines came under attack from 180 North

continued on page 94

Once inside the battleship, the sixteen-inch projectile must be removed from the hoist harness and placed on the projectile deck. This marks the end of an arduous loading process and the final step is taken with the usual care, attention and physical effort. Although *New Jersey* always had an adequate supply of projectiles, a directive from on high limited the battleship to sixty-five rounds per day during combat operations off the coast of Vietnam.

The tough job of stowing projectiles completed, an ordnanceman seems entitled to a brief respite. Long hours and hard work—not leisure—keynoted life aboard *New Jersey* during her Southeast Asia cruise, so interludes like this were infrequent.

The business end of the smaller five-inch guns aboard the *New Jersey* required attention as well as the main batteries.

*continued on page 91*

Vietnamese regulars; it was a nocturnal equivalent of the seige of the Alamo. A beleagered Marine called in the locations of the North Vietnamese, and *New Jersey* engaged with her five-inch batteries. During the long night, the battleship fired no fewer than 1,710 five-inch rounds. At dawn the port gun mounts were littered with empty powder casings and paint was scorched from gun barrels. Oceanview was saved from being overrun, and the effectiveness of naval gunfire in close support of ground forces was again proven. Ironically, the battlewagon's finest moment did not require the sixteen-inch guns.

The commendations that flowed into *New Jersey's* Command from field commanders in the region became too numerous to list. Cabled Admiral John J. Hyland, commander of Pacific forces, "Your whole performance has drawn . . . admiration. . . ." During early-1969, with one more rest stop at Subic, *New Jersey* remained on the gunline and poured in the fire. The men were unaware that those mysterious figures, the Higher Ups, had decided to end the combat cruise at the end of March.

*continued on page 100*

Spit and polish was the norm aboard the pristine *New Jersey*. Working on the big guns often required getting into unusual positions, but the ship's crew felt a genuine pride of purpose and enjoyed these chores.

The moment of truth. A target has been identified and, on orders, an ordnanceman has let loose by pulling the trigger, actually a brass handle inside the turrent. Contrary to what physics students might think, the guns fire over a longer distance when raised to maximum elevation. With a boom and an enormous flash from spent powder, a shell is sent on its way. The sound and recoil of the gun will be heard throughout the ship. The projectile is easily visible to the naked eye, leaving the gun and arching upward. Targets were usually too far away for crewmen to see the results of their work, but on occasion—as when attacking a troop concentration on the shoreline—they could watch the projectile throughout its entire trajectory, see the explosion on shore and hear the explosion several seconds later.

continued from page 94

Ordered back to Long Beach in April 1969, *New Jersey* was briefly diverted to Korea when the North Koreans shot down a US EC-121 reconnaissance plane, killing thirty-one men. She returned to Long Beach on May 5, 1969. Scheduled to return to the Vietnam gunline in August, she received a new skipper in a routine, scheduled change on August 27, 1969, when Captain Robert C. Peniston took the helm from Captain Snyder.

The ship was again armed and prepared to go into harm's way; Peniston was strongly motivated to inflict a new round of devastating blows to the North Vietnamese. Thus it was with nothing less than astonishment that the crew learned of a decision by Secretary of Defense Melvin Laird to deactivate *New Jersey* immediately. For budgetary reasons, the battleship would be sailed to Bremerton, Washington, and would be, to use Snyder's word, abandoned.

Peniston was no happier. It was an incredible decision. *New Jersey* had been deluged with praise for the effectiveness and striking power of her big guns. General Leonard Chapman, commandant of the Marine Corps, had noted that

continued on page 103

Ouch! Journalists were frequently aboard *New Jersey* including this October 2, 1968, occasion off the Vietnamese coast, and those without earplugs often used fingertips to gain relief from the roar of the guns.

continued from page 100

"Thousands of American lives were saved by the speed, accuracy and enormous penetration power of the battleship's heavy guns. Unlike B-52 bombers, tactical aircraft and Marine artillery, *New Jersey* was always there, day and night, in good weather or bad, and her guns were always ready for every target, whether a troop concentration or a fortified bunker. Just knowing that *New Jersey* was there bolstered the moral of our fighting Marines."

Thinking that he might be the last man in history to serve as skipper of a battleship, Captain Peniston took *New Jersey* to Bremerton on a sad and somber journey into the northwestern rain. Every man on board knew that it had been senseless to commission the great battlewagon for only one cruise and then mothball her again, but sailors follow orders. Peniston had been aboard *New Jersey* as an Annapolis midshipman in 1943 and as a newly commissioned ensign in 1946; he believed the ship could yet make an enormous

continued on next page

Even while readying for action in the war zone, *New Jersey* found some lighter moments and was able to host the Shipmate of the Month, Anne Morell. BB-62's crew had no difficulty obtaining permission to use the trademarked *Playboy* rabbit. Morell did not get atop the center main battery gun of turret 1 as easily as it appears, but crew members were glad to render assistance.

contribution in Vietnam. He was also aware of the pride and greatness of this huge gray lady. It seemed terribly sad that the only way to show pride was to do a superb job of deactivating the vessel.

The final journey for *New Jersey*'s gun projectiles occurred at Bremerton when they filled a twenty-six-car train. The battleship's crew did a fine job, deactivating the vessel in 100 days rather than the four months prescribed. On December 17, 1969, in a deliberately low-key ceremony snubbed by Secretary of the Navy John Warner, *New Jersey* was formally decommissioned.

When North Vietnam launched her Easter offensive on March 30, 1972, and American ships and warplanes again assaulted targets in the north, *New Jersey* was not available—and sorely missed. The great warship had been brought out of mothballs too late, and put back too early; it was widely believed that she might have helped turn the tide of the war otherwise.

On that gray day in Bremerton, as men held to their dignity but did not hold
continued on page 107

Night or day, dusk or dawn, *New Jersey* battered the foe. The glaring blast of each mighty gun, as seen here, was always followed by a smaller belch of smoke as the gun recoiled and returned to position. *New Jersey* men were especially proud that their accurate gunfire saved many lives among friendly ground forces.

*continued from page 104*
their tears, all in attendance believed that the last battleship had completed her last voyage.

They were wrong, as the 1980s have proven, and *New Jersey* serves in the fleet today. The vision lives.

The fiery muzzle flash has not yet had time to form during this daytime shoot as a sixteen-incher leaves the main battery gun.

The eye-dazzling muzzle flashes from the battleship's sixteen-inchers lasted for several seconds each time a round was fired. Rarely has *New Jersey*'s hull number been displayed with greater effect than here, the 62 atop turret 2 washed in a blaze of light while turret 1 unleashes a brilliant and noisy barrage from two of its three guns. Fire missions were almost always carried out with less than the dreadnought's full main battery of nine guns, since targets did not justify the full treatment while precision and accuracy were tantamount.

*Following pages*

With the bow of the vessel "buttoned up," *New Jersey* blasts away. To the gun captain and ordnancemen inside the turret, the target on a distant shore may be something of an abstraction—reported to them orally by plotters—but the work of bombarding an enemy has real, personal significance. The battleship often received visits from soldiers and Marines who had been helped in crucial land battles by the devastating naval fire support.

*Following pages*
*New Jersey*'s main battery guns take on an entrenched enemy. A split second before the arrival of a shell, enemy troops could hear it howling down on them. The destructive power of even a single shell was several times that of an air strike by a flight of fighter-bombers. Had *New Jersey* been used instead of aircraft during later periods in the war, after the battlewagon was prematurely returned to mothballs, the toll on the enemy might have been enormous. Captain Robert C. Peniston, who became the ship's second skipper during combat, believed The Big J could have made an even larger contribution, and was saddened by the task of returning the mighty battleship to Bremerton for retirement.

**Following pages**

At the December 17, 1969,
conclusion of her Vietnam-era
reincarnation—an untimely
conclusion, many felt, in view of
the ship's potential contribution to
a war that continued without her—
Captain Robert C. Peniston slid
*New Jersey* into mooring at
Bremerton, Washington. Perhaps
clairvoyant about the vessel's
future in the 1980s, Peniston did
not feel the story was over. The
ship would sleep lightly, he said,
"and hear the call, if again
sounded, to provide Firepower for
Freedom." Peniston knew he was
at the end of a chapter, not the end
of the story. *New Jersey*, he
predicted, "will hear the call. And
thanks to her crew, she is ready."